Alligator or Crocodile?

How Do You Know?

WHICH ANIMAL IS WHICH?

Melissa Stewart

Enslow Elementary
an imprint of

Enslow Publishers, Inc.
40 Industrial Road
Box 398
Berkeley Heights, NJ 07922
USA

http://www.enslow.com

Contents

Words to Know

jaw (JAW)—One of the two bones that make up an animal's mouth. Teeth grow out of the jaw.

mammal (MAA muhl)—An animal that has a backbone and lungs. It always has the same body temperature. It feeds its baby milk.

reptile (REP tyl)—An animal that has a backbone and lungs. Its body temperature is the same as the air around it. It lays eggs.

Do You Know?

Which of these reptiles is an alligator? Which one is a crocodile? Do you know?

Freshwater or Salt Water?

Alligators live in freshwater. Lakes, streams, and swamps have freshwater.

Crocodiles can live in freshwater. They can also live in salt water.

Rounded or Pointed Snout?

An alligator has a wide, rounded snout. It is shaped like the letter U. It can crush a turtle's shell.

A crocodile has a long, pointed snout. It is shaped like the letter V. It can chomp fish, birds, and **mammals.**

Wide or Narrow Jaw?

An alligator has a wide upper jaw. Its lower jaw is a little bit smaller. When an alligator's mouth is closed, you can see only its top teeth.

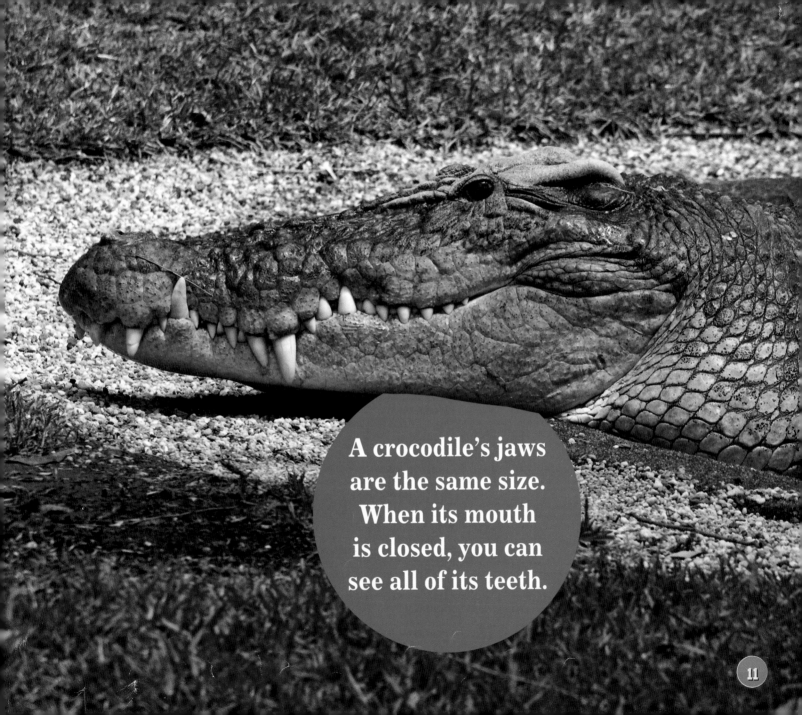

A crocodile's jaws are the same size. When its mouth is closed, you can see all of its teeth.

Dark or Light?

An alligator has dark skin. It looks black as it swims through the water.

A crocodile has lighter skin. It is usually a mix of green, gray, and brown.

Mound or Hole?

How does
a mother alligator
make a nest?
She piles up a mound
of plants near the
water. She lays
twenty to fifty eggs
in the nest.

A mother crocodile digs a nest near the water. Then she lays up to sixty eggs in the hole.

Mom Stays or Leaves?

A mother alligator takes care of her young for up to one year.

When young crocodiles hatch, their mother carries them to the water. Then she swims away.

Now Do You Know?

This animal lives in freshwater.

It has dark skin.

It takes care of its young.

Its nest is a mound of plants.

It has a wide, rounded snout.

Its upper jaw is wider than its lower jaw.

It's an alligator!

This animal can live in freshwater or salt water.

It has light, greenish-brown skin.

It has a long, pointed snout.

It does not take care of its young.

It digs a nest in the mud or sand.

Its jaws are the same size.

It's a crocodile!

What a Surprise!

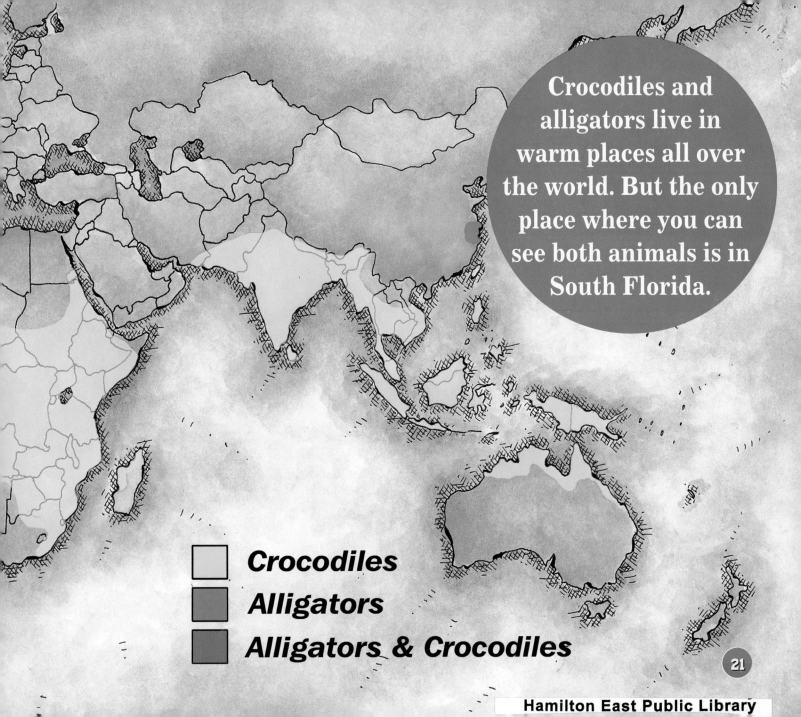

Crocodiles and alligators live in warm places all over the world. But the only place where you can see both animals is in South Florida.

Crocodiles
Alligators
Alligators & Crocodiles

21

Learn More

Books

Arnosky, Jim. *All About Alligators*. New York: Scholastic, 2008.

Beck, Paul. *Uncover a Crocodile*. San Diego: Silver Dolphin Books, 2006.

Gibbons, Gail. *Alligators and Crocodiles*. New York: Holiday House, 2010.

Tourville, Amanda Doering. *A Crocodile Grows Up*. Minneapolis, Minn.: Picture Window Books, 2007.

Web Sites

American Alligator
http://animals.nationalgeographic.com/
animals/reptiles/american-alligator.html

Crocodiles
http://www.pbs.org/wgbh/nova/crocs/

Reptiles: Alligator and Crocodile
http://www.sandiegozoo.org/animalbytes/
t-crocodile.html

Index

Enslow Elementary, an imprint of Enslow Publishers, Inc.

Enslow Elementary® is a registered trademark of Enslow Publishers, Inc.

Copyright © 2011 by Melissa Stewart

Library of Congress Cataloging-in-Publication Data

Stewart, Melissa.
Alligator or crocodile? : how do you know? / Melissa Stewart.
p. cm. — (Which animal is which?)
Includes bibliographical references and index.
Summary: "Explains to young readers how to tell the difference between alligators and crocodiles"—Provided by publisher.
ISBN 978-0-7660-3677-2
1. Alligators—Juvenile literature. 2. Crocodiles—Juvenile literature. I. Title.
QL666.C925S74 2011
597.98—dc22

2010003275

Paperback ISBN 978-1-59845-234-1
Printed in the United States of America
102010 Lake Book Manufacturing, Inc., Melrose Park, IL

10 9 8 7 6 5 4 3 2 1

To Our Readers: We have done our best to make sure all Internet Addresses in this book were active and appropriate when we went to press. However, the author and the publisher have no control over and assume no liability for the material available on those Internet sites or on other Web sites they may link to. Any comments or suggestions can be sent by e-mail to comments@enslow.com or to the address on the back cover.

♻ Enslow Publishers, Inc., is committed to printing our books on recycled paper. The paper in every book contains 10% to 30% post-consumer waste (PCW). The cover board on the outside of each book contains 100% PCW. Our goal is to do our part to help young people and the environment too!

Photo Credits: Artville, pp. 20–21; naturepl.com: © Adrian Davies, p. 16, © Anup Shah, p. 17; Photo Researchers, Inc.: E. R. Degginger, pp. 5, 19, Millard H. Sharp, pp. 4, 18, Nigel J. Dennis, p. 15; Shutterstock.com, pp. 1, 2, 3, 6, 7, 9, 10, 11, 12, 13; © Treat Davidon/FLPA/Minden Pictures, p. 14; © Yobro10/iStockphoto.com, p. 8.

Cover Photos: Shutterstock.com

Note to Parents and Teachers: The *Which Animal Is Which?* series supports the National Science Education Standards for K–4 science. The Words to Know section introduces subject-specific vocabulary words, including pronunciation and definitions. Early readers may need help with these new words.